My Little Book for the Soul

Messages from Spirit

DOLLY FOX

The Puttering Pen

Spokane Valley, WA

My Little Book for the Soul: Messages from Spirit

 The Puttering Pen

Published by The Puttering Pen
Spokane Valley, WA

ISBN 978-1-7363600-0-2

Free

I am Free, I am Me, I am You

Allow these words to be a bridge for you
to learn to truly find your way, to trust
who you really are and to discover

How good it feels to be you.

My purpose for this book was never
about me. I knew instantly it was about us.
It always felt like a grand dance
of self discovery…

A love letter for us.

My life brought me to this point in time
and my soul revealed what I had to share.
The words continue to speak to me.

I am 'you' on a path through this life.

Suffering is no longer an option.
It just doesn't belong to me anymore.

I am free. I am me. I am you.

HAPPINESS
DOESN'T CHANGE
HOW YOU FEEL
ABOUT GRIEF.

IT CHANGES
HOW YOU ENGAGE
WITH LIFE.

Further

Take your life further than you ever thought you could.

❀

A smile to a lonely face is the cosmic love of a mountain conquered. Begin with a smile.

❀

Pick up where someone could not do it themselves. It is like a trip to a foreign land. The landmarks and journeys are no different than what we can do for our brethren.

Make no mistake, the glossy travels of those that show you all they do is an empty plate when asked to share themselves on a level of sharing your most deeply felt pain that beckons to them to be released so you can go away feeling like you were held in their arms, just once when you needed it the most. Not their stories, not their possessions, not their endless musings. Just listen once to the person who needs your heart. Give it to them," just once" they ask. "Please listen to me, I need more then I can find inside, help me find it, listen just this once." Be that person, stop, listen, give of yourself. Not the life that has been filled with possessions of nothingness to the person in need of you.

Let us be kind. There is no cost. It is in us. It is there to give. It is for all of us.

We face the depths of our lives many times during this journey. We need each other for a second. Give that second.

It is the payload of our lives.

Hands

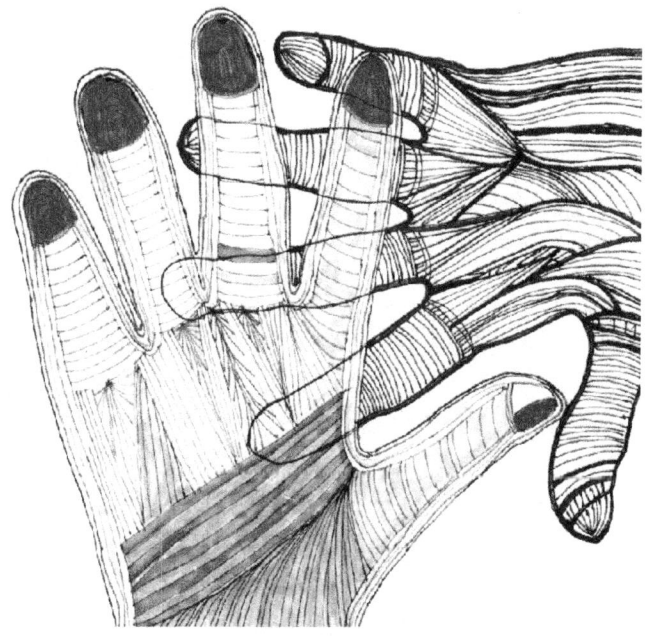

Take the hand that reaches out, take the hand and hold on like it is from the heavens reaching out to you and them. There is no difference between the one in need and the one that is there for you in need. It is the same. It is the breath and the glory of who we are. Take your own hand when you need it too. You are also the brethren that needs your heart to care for your aching heart.

❀

You are the love child of God. How good is that? Truly?

❀

The art of a handshake can make the world go round for eternity because of the loving energy that catapults it like a trampoline in the backyard.

Shelter your life in times of pain and let not others fuel your fears of loneliness. It is time unto yourself that if not kept in you, the gift in you, will not be present only to you, to be honored and shared when ready. It will be piece milled out like old gossip that has no place except to be discarded for the next phase of a scattered life that is not being lived but divided into aspects of all, except for the one it was meant to heal in time of need.

❀

Sad one day, happy the next. Use your sadness for your courage training and happy for the teacher in yourself. You are everything to you.

❀

We are alive because we need to be. It is our choice, yes, we choose this. Show it how much better you can show it.

❀

Broken minds and bodies are yours so others that see you, but not know you, can take part in your life and you will both be healed. The next time around you can then be the healer of the healed.

Rumi was a bearer of the spiritual word. You too are a "Rumi" of the day with the gifts of words and deeds.

❀

A diamond is beautiful but a smile untouchable in its beauty and worth. Wear your diamonds, but shine your smile, it could launch a thousand ships if need be.

When you engage in love, you always engage with the one that asked.

Clouds

The weather is but a chance for the clouds to say hello and the sky to say hello back.

❀

A beefy looking man, a skinny, skinny looking woman, how is that what we should attain? For what? For whom? How does it make this life better for us?

It doesn't, get over it.

❀

A shallow mind cannot be filled up, there is too much it needs. Fill an empty bucket where it counts in truth.

❀

The nectar of our lives will meet the sound of you. You will see and feel it in your breath, heartbeat and the sound that blows your deeds back for you to love yourself again.

❁

There is no hard labor needing to be done when the truth speaks its name. It dwells in all places, in all ways, in all spaces whether the sun shines or not.

❁

See the bright shadows of the magnificence of the beauty that lies within you and without anything but itself.

❁

Make your friends your checkmates that always win because they have you.

It is a double helix of joy when you have people to share your most intimate and crazy life happenings. Do not make them your step stool to listen to your grievances and noisy bickering's found like garbage throughout your day.

Use them to make you feel, *really feel*, like you are supposed to, deeply and with abandoned feelings that we can share, laugh at, cry at.

❀

We must learn to bring ourselves to recognize who we are in others. Build up each other. Stop using people as a platform of the ilk of what you want them to give you.

Give them first and you will forever be the recipient of their love they didn't know they had or shared.

❀

The I Am needs nothing new, the movement of life is the spark that ignites it.

Be thankful for you, because you are the thankless holder of all your past miseries that ask you to turn your head away from and into the one that held on to all the love that finds its way into the light.

❀

Now is not the time to wonder about what can or cannot be decided if or when one should walk the distance or not. Now is the time for you and me to witness the fine beauty that lays ahead of all our dreams and expectations that will come and go but will be meant with honor and glory because of that the traveling it has done to get to the place where it should be.

❀

When you ask for anything, anything will give you what you most need. When in doubt, ask doubt to find itself and then it will be released.

❀

Use the hand, the hand that holds the baby's and old men for help when you have a hand to share and a heart that needs mending.

Use your hand and reach out to those that linger in the doorways, alleyways, the street corners and under bridges. Let them not see a harsh comment but an answer to the desire to be humbled and loved by the experience of the passerby.

❀

It does not get any better then the present moment, which in turn has the next moment to experience and ponder. Do not resist the pull of gravity that propels you to keep going on and on.

❀

When connected to the earth, you are the catalyst to all there ever has been.

The morning mist is the showing off its dressing up for you.

Sun

When the sun shines and you are not aware of the miracle of it all, come away with all that you desire, for the sun shines for you and the stars are bright for you and the grass is green for you.

Do not forget that you are the one that lingers in the heavens and earth. Do not wonder what is, just be. Just be that person that wanders in the green grass of heaven and earth.

On a cloudy day rest assure that the clouds are steppingstones to the gods and goddesses, the angels, the master and those that seek refuge from the trouble of who and what they see below themselves. They know that the clouds are the blanket of warmth and love when all is in balance with above and soon below.

The clouds are but an extension of what you see when everything around is in harmony to it.

❀

Animals are the representation of the true power and not the false notion of mans dominion over them. They have ruled with love and acceptance of themselves and stayed steadfast in who they are and what they came to do.

❀

When the lights go out and there is nobody to talk to but you and the fear of loneliness descends upon you, there is nothing time will not bring to you but the love that is yours to have and share only to you. The lonely hours are to spend for you and you alone to reveal your best laid plans. Your hopes and dreams are not lost to you but put-on hold until you awaken from your dark slumber.

❀

Now is not the time to wish and wonder. For wish and wonder are like the frosting on a stale cupcake. They both look and feel like they are fresh and good but it is only a manifestation of nothing.

Make a wish, set it free and when it comes you will realize that the wish was only a passing fancy that did not excite you as much as you anticipated.

❧

Dark days, dark nights and dark dreams are the invitation to find out what the light is all about.

❧

The fire is a coal of the world in which we never owned and never will. As you do not or never will own the rock, the blade of grass or your neighbors' fence. When the morning comes crawling over the mountains, the forest and the seas, it is ours to love and care for as much as you would the air you breath and the love you have for the smell of a newborn.

When the sun shines, when the clouds billow, sit with them as they cross the sky. Be the wonder when they gaze at your marvelous self. They love the way you look and smile at their beauty too.

We are all in this as a whole.

❀

When the night comes crawling along on its nightly quest, let the sum of all parts rise to the occasion of understanding and knowing from the fruits of the days labor. Let in the next light of day and sing a song of joy when the sun goes down and the moon takes over its duties. Then sleep with the stars and know that you will be riding on a cloud of clear visions of the new awakenings where you will find joy and the things that light up when the morning comes.

When the stars start to rise and shine, we will never know what we can do and what we are not supposed to do now or ever.

❀

Let the birds fly and the leaves fall and the worms dig. Find the rich soil of earth and walk without the promise of fear that hides in your mind trapped in the tight cocoon of falsehoods. Find your bird and fly in the sky and drop love along the way.

The quiet sun, the noisy clouds, the sweet moon, the pitter pattering of rain and the heart that beats to the rhythm of its very existence.

Heartbeat

Sadness is when the soul feels its heartbeat. Love yourself anyway, all aspects of self, love, hate, anger, guilt, frustration, loneliness, resentment… love those things and it will change the energy of yourself.

❀

Together let us be all the things the next in line needs when your heart is bursting from the good deed done. Know the universe was held in its highest form and you were a part and just as magnificent as a star, moon, ocean or mountain that looks to each other with the knowledge that is was always there for you and has always been there to marvel at the glorious beauty that is held in all.

❀

When will it happen you ask? When will it stop you ask? When will it feel better you ask? When will I get my chance you ask?

Maybe it did happen or stopped or was better and the chance was there. It will come again just like the years of our lives and the changing landscape of who, what and how we see things. So, will the "when".

❁

The world is a reflection of what we do and think. If love were expanded and given out from all on a daily visit, there would be no 'want'. What a world that would be, united, whole, happy, comforting, humane, stable and a oneness like nothing we can comprehend.

It will happen but we can accelerate it if we can possibly just love ourselves first. It is not selfish. It is the most courageous thing you will ever do for you.

❁

When all is done, dwell not on the feeling of accomplishment but in the knowing of a job well done by the one that dwells in the heart of all of us.

Honor all your experiences and allow these words to be the love letter you always wanted to write. Know it was always you that held the pen, held the paper and held the world you wanted to be in.

When all is well, it is time to bask in the glory of yourself, not to deny the memory by thinking otherwise.

❀

The soul is a book not written, the steps not taken, the words not spoken and the hunger that has not been nourished. Open it up, let it in, say hello and let it be all that it came to show you.

❀

In order for the world to change, it must be one heart at a time and we can do it all if we have people willing to see themselves as agents of change.

We all have the capacity, all of us, dark, light or in between. Our shadows are just shadows of misunderstandings that can change faster then all the years it took to get there.

❀

Miracles are within us, use them, big or small, they are for us.

So many things are here for us. We can stop listening to ourselves long enough to hear the messages that blow in. Our breath is the miracle of life but there are so many small and beautiful ones to us that we do not see.

Let us look closer you and I. We can meet in the middle.

Somewhere in our souls there is a place for a picnic. The basket is full and we are hungry. The thirst we have for love, understanding and recognition for our journey can be acknowledged ourselves by acknowledging the very thing that acknowledges us, our inner desire for more love.

❀

Enjoy your life, see things that are there in front of you but not seen by the skeptics. Be your own scientist and see the molecules of life in its truest form. Be your own teacher and learn what fills you with love and joy and how to experience sadness within yourself.

❀

You can be those things and more. You were born to be here, not anywhere you are told to go. Ask and the question becomes the answer.

How can you be anything but what you are? But what you are doesn't know what that means. The self-reflection is a window into what there can be. Go further and deeper until the reflection comes alive and you then know yourself.

❀

When the flow of life is just that, it always moves ahead even when you are facing the other way.

❀

You have not lost anything that was not yours or is not yours to hold onto forever. Leave it.

Look ahead. That is where the treasure is to be found. Maybe after the rapids, maybe a little further down stream, maybe along the rocky shore and maybe straight ahead.

Life is one of many and how you perceive it is tantamount. Look at a tree and how many lives it holds in its branches.

Seek not to be of service but to be service and you will have no need to seek anything. Your true service serves you every second of everyday without even trying and look not to where it is but look to the holder of knowledge with love, respect and reverence, which is your soul.

When the dog comes home, give a bone. When you come home, give yourself a bone too. We all need things to chew on.

❀

A cactus and all its prickly sides are as
beautiful and vital as the velvety side of a rose
but both have thorns to show where they have
been and how hard they work.

❀

Troubles are stepping stones to higher
ground and a skinned ego is one less hold
on you.

❀

We are people, angry, scared, lonely and
everything that you can think you are and are

not. Think of your gifts instead which aren't
some special feature your body thinks is better
then others.

Not true.

The '*you*' is what you must see. Look closer
even though you have been told by you or to you.
You have the right to love yourself.

Do not dismiss your crown that is in your space of life. You are the bearer and secret love of all that you are. Carry it with dignity and see how straight you walk and see the colors ahead, around and on you.

❀

Marry anyone but don't expect them to be an extension of you. Like flowers in the garden, they will grow at a rate only understood to them. They are not yours to power over or set on a high stool.

Let them walk their path that leads them and be a friend to their existence. You can free both of yourselves to be by the side of the one you love.

❀

Nurture not the romance but the company of the existence.

Injure not your neighbor, for they are here and you are there. They are your brethren to help you see that the imperfection of life is a rule of engagement for you to move past and forward to free yourself from the frustration of your imperfection also.

❀

Treat the birds and all animals like you would a beloved friend. We are not here to be above them or them below us. Our connection to all has been given to us as a tool to see aspects of all that can be.

❀

Leaves of trees are nothing more then the extension of their growth and when they fall it is their way of saying, I am ready to let go so I can metamorphosis into something new upon the earth.

Candles

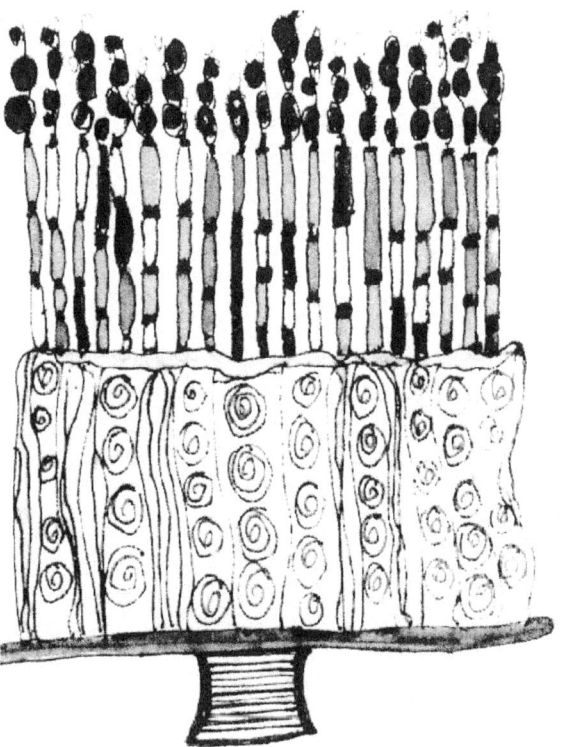

Light a candle, make a wish and therein lies the promise of each and every one of us, the desire to be held in the arms of ourselves. Light a candle again and the flicker is you watching the light in you.

It is the birthday of a new you. It is the culmination of your labor pains. You are like no other. You are the son and daughter of the universe. Born to shine your light for those that come to you with broken wings.

You were born to be here. It is a manifestation of the karma that has been bestowed to us. Every detail has been offered for your journey. Be happy, take what you are and make it into a gift unto yourself.

You will look back at all the squandered moments of times past and know how it did not work for you. Make it work for you now.

When you look from the heavens and see all the beloveds you will understand it all.

Understand it all while standing on earth. You can do it.

❀

The lights are the impulses of our lives to be not what we think but to be who we really are. In the quiet, maybe sad night, it is when we can see not the made-up stories of a corporation on television, written words or whatever else is for sale. You are not for sale and those that are may they be set free by the hands and minds that bounds them. Lift up your spirit to reach the clouds, the stars and then your very birthplace.

❀

Get outside your head space. The world is bursting with people and yet loneliness is a scourge that has a need that begs to be filled. Can we find a way to enter that space?

Loneliness is a disease of our perception of how life is lived. Learn how to live, ask your inner-being what you can do. It will answer when you do not even hear it.

❁

Now is not the time to wish and wonder, it's the time to wonder and watch the wish come true.

Only when you play, putter, skip, dance, smile or lounge around, the things that make you part and parcel to the feelings of being happy. You can extend it if you do those things, whether standing or not. How much better to feel that inner momentum as you.

You can and will find yourself and what makes it so glorious. But it might take many lifetimes. Why not now, today, this very moment in time?

❁

There are people who need you, need you in the only way you can show them who they really are and the gift to them, by being you.

❈

The shiny lights on a Christmas tree shows its brilliance but the boughten strand from the store, your lights are not.

❈

Being tired, being hungry, being tired, being hungry, two things that feel the best. When tired and hungry, sleep and eat, the good times.

❈

Fill the bottles for the car, fill the watering jug, fill the tub with enough for you and lest you have more, find a cup, fill it up and then sit on the couch, the day is done.

❈

Find the fox hole and leave it alone. The next time the fox hole might find you and then all hell breaks loose.

❀

Now more then ever, let yourself be who you are and who you want to be and not a carbon copy of who you thought.

Will you not see yourself as the gift under the tree, the out cropping on the couch or soaking in the tub? You do not have to be anything that glows so bright on the cover or inside the glossy photos of people and lives that are not real and put there for you to market yourself as unworthy. You are not for sale, the gloss is!

❀

When you meet that person that walks by you and your eyes meet with the beauty of your heart, know that you are a treasure in the highest way.

❀

The awakening comes when you have found your potential and just that thought alone assures you, you are All That Is. Nothing else gets in the way because the road, journey or way,

is already understood as its never desiring grace
because it is always there and understood
to be so.

❀

When the time comes to be around what you
are and what you are not, then you will be at the
highest level of freedom to you and all those that
come to you for the necessary tools to carry it
out.

It only takes one that spreads to many.

❀

When the angels begin to access the self-
imposed damage inflicted upon ones own soul,
first is a song of wonder and love. Wonder for
how you managed to get so skinned up and love
for the arrival of a large Band-aid®.

❀

Saying 'thank you' is your way of saying that
you honor what was given to you and in return

you 'thank' yourself for the gift that you can never have too many of.

❀

The signs are there but the direction you see is not the one to follow. Look again and again and the arrow gets bigger each time until your soul speaks to you in the quiet hour of your pain and shows the way so you will no longer carry the burden of not knowing.

❀

The direction was always there but the cloud of life took longer then you thought. Once found is never lost again.

❀

Candles burn, hearts break, crows caw, birds sing, dogs howl and the moon says hello back.

Sunflowers

In all things give thanks and gratitude because in all things are we.

❀

Trust yourself more then anything or anybody, ever. You are the master of your universe and you serve the highest of the high, you. Without hesitation be you, honor you, love you, cradle you, rock you, nurture you and all the people around will reap all the rewards that come pouring forth from your very soul. Think only of what loving you, can and will do.

❀

Go gently, swiftly, with rage in your soul for the nectar of the beauty of the next journey.

❀

Choose you, choose all, choose noise, rage, hurt, and anger because when it comes crawling along your way, it is meant to be greeted by acceptance and a desire to find the truth of itself, not to be despised for the yearnings that are on their way on the back of a rocky stone you ride.

But stay on, stay you, stay in constant reverence for you are no different then mankind. We are all one.

The world is a reflection of what we do and think. If love were expanded and given out from all on a daily visit, there would be no 'want'. What a world that would be, united, whole, happy, comforting, humane, stable and a oneness like nothing we can comprehend.

It will happen, but we can accelerate it if we can possibly just love ourselves first. It is not selfish, it is the most courageous thing you will ever do for you.

A butterfly is beautiful to behold, the colors, the soft flight of its wings, the way it sails through the air. It is a gift of beauty to you. A thousand people may witness the same beauty but you will see it all for you and just you.

Longing is the thought of past fears desiring to be future promises. The night is but the answer to the day.

❀

Who said life would feel good from the moment of birth anyways? It is a journey fraught with many things. Every life you have will ask of you things that are not meant to consume but you do and do and do, until the doing becomes clear to you that it's a road to the heavens. Give thanks for the hard, sad and lonely journey.

The mountain is your love child and it becomes clearer how absolutely amazing you are to have traveled so far and worked so hard to overcome so much. Once you own your journey as yours and yours alone, you will know these words to be true. It was never about 'them'; it was for you. You never would have made the journey and found the golden glow of you without them.

Acknowledge them as you were part of theirs too. You will meet again and you will be able to hold your differences in a light of love and admiration and joy that was never felt before.

❀

The answer lies not in the knowing but in the trusting of the knowing. The mirror shows but a small reflection but the soul is the mirror that reflects the whole of you.

❀

The holidays come and go and the cookies are made and eaten but the plate remains the same. It is your joy, your soul and your very body that turns out the energy of life. The heartbeat of your soul puts out notes of longing and love. Make it about healing your brothers and sisters too and you will be recognized as the angel in human form that we pray to the heavens for when we want to see the beauty of our world.

❀

Hate is the misconception of an ego that man has allowed to rule and conquer his very soul. If you want to unchain your heart, let it go places that you never thought possible. People will see you for the person you are, not the person that secretly thinks you should be.

❀

Songs, everyone everywhere, every sound is a song. Listen to the leaves when the wind blows through. The sounds of the infinite songs of the universe.

❀

Inside the walls of justice lies the rules-of-engagement to the beginnings of what man has produced and cannot control or neither does he have the power. The power is there to benefit mankind, not to use as a tool of engagement.

❀

The animals dwell in a constant flow of life and should be revered for all their hard work and contribution to the earths balance.

❀

The morning mist is the showing off its dressing up for you.

Go directly to the one that cannot see the future for fear it will bring nothing good to the table, but instead look at what the table is. A new manifestation of the abundance that is always present as a buffet of food set forth on the table with the pretty napkins.

Manifests ask for nothing and everything because the nothing is always there to be turned into everything you hoped and prayed for. The nothing awaits for the invitations to be invited in.

Wonder

You must see yourself to experience the chills of wonderment.

❀

You are not alone; loneliness makes you feel lonely. So many times, during your lifetime it is there like the storm in your heart or the pain in your body or the misunderstanding of what we are to do when the instructions are nowhere to be read. When life overwhelms us to the point of longing to be someone and somewhere else, when who we wish to love are yearnings that are like dried up leaves on a Christmas tree left to be discarded for the promise of more hugs next year.

❀

To be understood on a level that we crave is inside us all. We are our own love child. The hugs we cried for, the nurturing we could never find, the joy that was never found but thought it was promised from the echoes of the hollow hallways. Love yourself. It will bring tears to your eyes and a warmth in your understanding of who you are.

Do not deny your secret self, it is meant for you to birth into who and what you can be at any given moment. You are the hidden treasure that lays amongst the kings and queens, the beggars, the lost, the found and reborn. Like the stars in the sky, only you can tell your story. Show it life and what can be.

Do not waste yourself in the chatter and darkness of idle living. Turn on the light, see who you are, see what there is for you. See how you can show yourself the way.

❀

The sun will shine when the earth is no longer here for you but will shine on and on. Like the sky that can never not be, it is you too that will go on and on without the earth to stand upon. The heavens are yours to comfort and love you.

You will see everything that was and will be. Make this time one of respect for you and your brethren no matter what they look like outside, for you will meet them in heaven and they will be beautiful to behold.

❀

Discover not what you are, but who you are, when no one is watching.

The manuscript of our lives is the same manuscript that God used for the soul to come open its pages and show us how to write our story new each day. It is meant to not repeat the chapter but to revel in the beauty in page after page.

❀

The angels are you. They are aspects of your true nature. We are all and can be angels to ourselves and those that roam the streets searching for the homeland that is theirs.

❀

Color, the art of life forms. Born of crystals, sunshine, stars, dust and the gleam in our eyes.

Be the watcher of your life, the all that you can watch. Everyone deserves to see themselves but rarely do for the self-centered back talk. You are not the person who needs scolding from you.

Pick yourself up and be that person who resided in the space and time of you. When in doubt, cast your troubles to the ground and let the ocean of your essence build a wall against the tide of your misunderstanding.

Ask and the question becomes the answer.

❀

Shoes cover feet, clothes cover your bodies and the soul needs nothing to cover it but to ask and covers itself by reaching itself and knowing that it is always covered with your hopes, dreams and desires. The soul is the spark that needs nothing but the realization of your soul to ignite it.

❀

When sleep is a distant desire, ask not why, but use the time to say goodnight, good day, hello and what can I do for you. The energy of love is the only energy that awakens the liberation to allow your body, mind and soul to play and sing to its own symphony. Only when you do not need or want answers to your souls calling is because the answer was always there but did not see its own self.

❀

When gratitude is spoken, the stars can feel the opening of light that waits for the mutation. Gratitude is saying 'thank you' and 'please come again' but knowing the next time you speak those words it will have manifested into a new and robust emotion not felt like the first time because its sweet nature allows it to grow.

❀

The animals will always be animals no matter what they do. Souls will always be souls no matter what you do. Hence, it is meant to be part of our lives.

❀

Do not judge yourself, it only makes your armor more difficult to remove. It only sees the armor on others when they do not see it on themselves. Why make another person pay for your lack of loving yourself. Once you know and feel it in your heart you will set yourself free and in turn be a catalyst to set your brethren free also.

❀

Silence is the release of your discarded noise.

Dance the night away, however you do and when your feet hurt and your body is worn, change your shoes and turn off the music. Job well done.

Wind

The howling wind has messages in its voyage. The love inside us all is hiding in plain sight. Make it your resolution to feel it. It is so much more glorious then you ever thought.

❀

Now, this moment in time, is what you have been given as a love token from the heavens. Do not wonder, ponder or want it to go away. Trust that it will appear again and again. A moment is just that. If you make one moment your love partner then the next moment will be the exchange of you and it.

Rest when you are tired, sad, overwhelmed and over worked. Take your time to be with you and be good to yourself. A hurried life does not make you a better person. But it can also show you how in need of your self-nutrition you have denied yourself for the sake of nothing.

❀

The crown on one's head is made of the same metal in earrings, jewelry and ornaments. That is all. Where you place it or even if you do not have any or want any, it is a false assumption of something more important then you really are, a child of God. Everyone is meant to help everyone, crown or no crown.

❋

The winter solstice is a time to allow nature to rest and, regroup and nurture themselves with love that is never questioned but always understood. Be who and how they become the nurturers of our planet. The cleansers of the air, home for the safety of animals, the beauty to behold for us, all without being asked, being driven, cajoled or enslaved, to be the grounding servant of our world.

❋

All the wise and wonderful words spoken and written are the same words that are in all of us. Find that wisdom, we need to hear it in our times of discomfort when we need it. You are your brother's soulmate in times of duress.

No guns needed, just your words or deeds, simple and beautiful.

Be a friend, be a light, be a master, a tear, song or a passing fancy. Oh, the things that we can be, it's so possible. Nature loves all, a person next to us will hug us when we need it most. Beauty from nature is no different. But love for us and itself serves in a different way. Shade, shelter, food, for all and the list goes on and on.

Do you understand how we all need each other?

❀

Dawn is the beginning of each day. A day is the beginning of each dawn, one and the same as with time. It is a never-ending cycle of the rotation of our lives.

Why continue to recycle each dawn with the same news and newspaper that is set-up for us to be in fear and anger over, it is not about our well-being. It is about the well-being of the marketing machine that pumps out garbage to make us come back for more and the money pours into them like a tidal wave.

But take a closer look at your gullibility of soaking up garbage that washed in each day through the media. The machine you know the truth of them, the rest just thinks you do. There is no honor to behold just the sucking sounds of your soul.

Wisdom is a definition not meant for scholars or the rich and famous. It is the energy of the ages that is inherent inside us all. Wise counsel is the breath you take, the step you take or how you are when you don't even know it.

The answers dwell in places gift wrapped in pretty paper and a bow only the angels could make. You are the tree, the ornaments and the recipient. Dig deep inside and you will find them, one after another. Don't believe it? You will after you find the very first one. The love it has will make you want to never, ever, look anywhere.

❀

It's about finding the wonder again, the one we leave behind on our way ahead but the ahead is only the behind. We just misinterpreted it as a different set of rules which we all know that now.

So, let's go and find it and see what we did with it and why, so we can get a piece of it. But we can of course.

Look not outside, but in you. Sounds hard but its you, no matter how you don't want to look. Look, look and look, just don't stop. It is the best work, pain and misery and love you will ever experience.

Courage my friend and have faith in yourself. Do what makes you feel good inside. It is worth it, it is how people feel love, real love, the love that resides in all beauty because it can't do otherwise, be you.

❀

Go not where others tell you to make your life your own. Make your world your own, it belongs to them and it belongs to all. Every person has the capacity to make it a wonderful, exciting, compassionate and marvelous life when you make it yours.

Why would you make it anything but? When you buy a house, car or refrigerator, do you not desire it to be all those things you want it to be? Then why ask anything less then those things that will always sustain you?

❀

Winter is given to all on earth, whether used as a metaphor or you live in a state of the changing equinox. Trees go to shed their beauty to rest for the next cycle of showing its beauty. Like the trees, rest and take refuge for yourself so you can be the beauty, see the beauty and share the beauty too.

❀

Death is its desire from its own limitations.

The nothing awaits for the invitation to be invited in.

❀

It is alright to look at the sun and the darkness as told by the sages and old men in the shadows of the barren trees. The ground moves with the wind. What you can see is the movement of everything that brings life the loud and noisy sound of nothing, to show how one sees the world and the colors of silence.

There are no colors in the idle hours of chatter from those that are filling their souls with bunches of nothing, but to be reborn with nothing and more nothing until the emptiness of hunger for more shout outs to listen to me with my colors of your beauty and the noise of your breath and grandeur of the beauty awaiting to see it all for you and just you. No anger, none of the damning of loneliness that envelope you like a tightrope and a hunger that never subsides.

The quiet of the snow, it absorbs the sounds of whispers. Be gentle with your words. The snow deserves to absorb nothing but the best from you. It only thinks of you. Do the same in your life. Allow the absorption of your beautiful thoughts.

Nurture yourself as you would the dying plant that needs water or a dog that begs for more. He that loves itself, loves the one who holds the watering bowl.

When the time comes to be around what you are and what you are not, then you will be at the highest level of freedom to you and all those that come to you for the necessary tools to carry it out. It only takes one that spreads to many.

Music

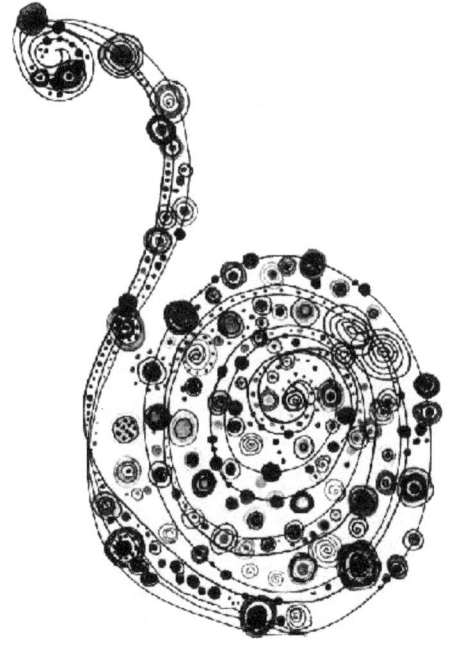

When you see the birth of yourself in ways that marvel and bring tears of relief, you will then see the steps in plain view to climb when courage of change finds it way to you all shiny and helpful even though your body sees the steps as a challenge that has been done before but yearns for more because it sees the top, and the top sees the top, and there sits the music.

Congratulations!

You are so awesome
Always were, now you know.

Celebrate!
Give it away

It will keep coming and coming...

It's a symphony that
never, ever, runs out of breath.

About the Author

A wounded heart has no where to go
except to find its way back, and when it
does, that is when the magic happens
because love can grow once again.

Dolly Fox is a lifelong resident of Spokane, Washington. After retiring, she picked up a pen and has never stopped since.

Made in the USA
Monee, IL
29 March 2021

63240372R00049